Round the World in Eighty Days

Jules Verne

Level 2

Retold by Michael Dean
Series Editors: Andy Hopkins and Jocelyn Potter

Pearson Education Limited
Edinburgh Gate, Harlow,
Essex CM20 2JE, England
and Associated Companies throughout the world.

Pack ISBN: 978-1-4058-8441-9
Book ISBN: 978-1-4058-8394-8
CD-ROM ISBN: 978-1-4058-8393-1

First Penguin Readers edition published 2000
This edition published 2008

3 5 7 9 10 8 6 4 2

Text copyright © Penguin Books Ltd 2000
This edition copyright © Pearson Education Ltd 2008
Illustrations by Fabián Mezquita
The author has asserted his moral right in accordance with the
Copyright Designs and Patents Act 1988

Set in 12/15.5pt A. Garamond
Printed in China
SWTC/02

Produced for the Publishers by AC Estudio Editorial S.L.

Published by Pearson Education Ltd in association with Penguin Books Ltd,
both companies being subsidiaries of Pearson Plc

For a complete list of the titles available in the Penguin Active Reading series please write to your local
Pearson Longman office or to: Penguin Readers Marketing Department, Pearson Education,
Edinburgh Gate, Harlow, Essex CM20 2JE, England.

Contents

1.1 What's the book about?

Look at the front of the book and at the pictures in the book. Then circle the right answers. Sometimes, there is more than one right answer.

1 The story is about ...

    a a journey.   **b** two lovers.   **c** a killer.

2 At the time of the story it is ...

    a 1773.   **b** 1873.   **c** 1973.

3 In the story, people go on journeys by ...

    a train.   **b** boat.   **c** bicycle.

4 The people in the story go to ...

    a India.   **b** Russia.   **c** the United States.

5 The people in the story have ...

    a no problems.   **b** some problems.   **c** a lot of problems.

1.2 What happens first?

Look at the names of Chapters 1 and 2, and at the words in *italics* below them. Then look at this picture. Answer the questions.

1 In the picture, which man is Phileas Fogg? ....

2 Is Phileas Fogg rich? ....

3 Is Passepartout a friend of Phileas Fogg? ....

4 What is 'The Bet', do you think? ....

CHAPTER 1

Phileas Fogg and Passepartout

'I want to forget the name "Passepartout".'
'I'll call you Passepartout,' said Phileas Fogg.

In 1872, the Reform **Club** in London's Pall Mall was a club for men only. Phileas Fogg went to the Reform Club every day. He left his house at 7 Savile Row at 11.30 in the morning and walked to the club. He had his lunch and his dinner there. He read the papers at the club, and he played cards. He left late in the evening and walked back to Savile Row. He went to bed at midnight.

Phileas Fogg was a cold man. He didn't talk much, and nobody knew much about him. But everything in his life had to be right. His washing water had to be at 31°C – not 30°C and not 32°C.

At 9.37 on the morning of 2nd October 1872 his **servant**, James Forster, brought him water at 30°C, not 31°C. So this servant had to go. Phileas Fogg sat at home in his Savile Row house. He waited for his new servant.

club /klʌb/ (n) A *club* is a building or a number of people. The people in a *club* are interested in the same things.
servant /ˈsɜːvənt/ (n) A *servant* lives and works for you in your house.

The new servant came. He was about thirty years old.

'You are French,' said Phileas Fogg, 'and your name is John?'

'No,' said the new servant. 'My name is Jean, Mr Fogg. They call me Jean Passepartout, because in French a "passepartout" can open every door. When things are bad, I can always get out. I can get out of anything!'

'Tell me about your work,' said Phileas Fogg.

'I am a good man and I can do a lot of different jobs,' said Jean Passepartout. 'I was a fireman in Paris. And ... look!' Passepartout did a high jump, then put his left leg and then his right leg on his head. He was a strong man.

'But I left France in 1867,' said Passepartout, 'and I came to England. I want to be a servant. I am looking for a quiet life. People say that you are the quietest man in Britain. So I want to work for you. I want to live quietly now. I want to forget the name "Passepartout".'

'I'll call you Passepartout,' said Phileas Fogg. 'What time is it?'

Passepartout pulled out a big watch and looked at it.

'It is 11.29, Mr Fogg,' he said.

'All right. From now, 11.29 on 2nd October 1872, you are my servant.'

With those words, Phileas Fogg put on his hat and went out. There was nobody in the house, then, only Passepartout.

'Here I am,' the Frenchman thought. 'But what do I do?'

He went into every room in the house. He found his room, and in it there was a **timetable**. Everything was there, starting from 8 o'clock. Phileas Fogg got up at that time.

8.23 Bring tea.
9.37 Bring washing water (31°C).
11.30 PF goes to the Reform Club.

Then, from 11.30 in the morning to midnight, everything was on the timetable. Mr Fogg always went to bed at midnight.

Passepartout smiled. 'This is right for me,' he thought. 'Mr Fogg is the man for me!'

timetable /ˈtaɪmˌteɪbəl/ (n) A *timetable* shows the times when trains, buses, boats or aeroplanes leave.

CHAPTER 2

The Bet

'We are leaving in ten minutes for Dover and Calais,' said Phileas Fogg.
'We are going round the world.'

It was 6.10 in the evening at the Reform Club. Phileas Fogg was in the card room. He was at a card table with the same five men as yesterday and the day before and the day before that.

Phileas Fogg and the five men didn't usually talk when they played cards. But this evening, before the game started, the men talked about a newspaper story. A **thief** walked into the Bank of England and took fifty-five thousand pounds. Then he walked out again. One of the men at the card table, Ralph, had a very good job at the Bank of England.

'They'll catch the man,' Ralph said. 'The best detectives are at every **port**. They know that the man is tall. He wears expensive clothes. They'll find him.'

'Oh, I don't know,' said Stuart, another man at the table. 'The world is a very big place.'

thief /θiːf/ (n) A *thief* takes things from people or buildings. *Thieves* don't pay for things or give them back.
port /pɔːt/ (n) A *port* is a place by the sea. Ships arrive and leave from there.

'It *was* a big place,' said Phileas Fogg.

'What do you mean – "was"? Is it smaller now?' said Stuart.

'Yes,' said Ralph. 'I think Mr Fogg is right. You can go round the world more quickly now.'

'All right,' said Stuart. 'You can go round the world in about three months, but that doesn't mean ...'

'Not three months,' said Phileas Fogg. 'Eighty days.'

'Fogg's right,' said Ralph. 'The Rothal to Allahabad **railway**, in India, is open now. Look – today's *Times* has a timetable for a journey round the world.' And he showed them, on the centre page of the paper.

London to Suez – railway and ship	*7*	*days*
Suez to Bombay – ship	*13*	*"*
Bombay to Calcutta – railway	*3*	*"*
Calcutta to Hong Kong – ship	*13*	*"*
Hong Kong to Yokohama – ship	*6*	*"*
Yokohama to San Francisco – ship	*22*	*"*
San Francisco to New York – railway	*7*	*"*
New York to London – ship and railway	*9*	*"*
	80	*days*

'Yes,' said Stuart, 'eighty days. It's all right on paper. But a lot of things can happen in eighty days. They can stop you on the way.'

'No, they can't, Mr Stuart,' said Phileas Fogg.

'Well, why don't you try, Mr Fogg?'

'Go round the world in eighty days?' said Phileas Fogg. 'All right. I have twenty thousand pounds in Baring's Bank. I'll **bet** all of it.'

'Twenty thousand pounds!' cried Ralph. 'Something will happen on the journey, and you'll lose all your money.'

---

railway /ˈreɪlweɪ/ (n) Trains run on *railways*. *Railway* companies sell tickets for their trains.
bet /bet/ (v/n) You *bet* money because you want to win more money. You win when something happens. You lose when you are wrong.

'Nothing will stop me,' Phileas Fogg said.

In the end, Phileas Fogg's five friends took the bet.

'Each person will pay you four thousand pounds – that's twenty thousand pounds – when we see you again here in the Reform Club in eighty days at the end of your journey round the world,' said Ralph. 'Or you have to pay us twenty thousand pounds. That's the bet.'

Phileas Fogg thought for a minute. 'Today is Wednesday, 2nd October. So I have to be back here, in this room in the Reform Club, on Saturday, 21st December at 8.45 in the evening.'

At 7.25, Phileas Fogg said good night to his friends and left the Reform Club. At 7.50, he opened the door of his house in Savile Row and went in.

'Mr Fogg? Is that you?' said Passepartout. He looked at the timetable. This was not on the timetable.

'We are leaving in ten minutes for Dover and Calais,' said Phileas Fogg. 'We are going round the world.'

Passepartout's eyes opened wide – very wide. He opened his arms then jumped on one leg.

'Round the world!' he said.

'In eighty days,' said Phileas Fogg. 'We have to go now. Now!'

'But your bags?'

'I'm not taking any bags. Well, one small bag. We can buy things on the way. Bring down my coat. Wear strong shoes. Move!'

At 8 o'clock, Passepartout was ready with a small bag. 'A quiet life,' he thought. 'Where is my quiet life?'

Phileas Fogg was ready. He had a book under his arm – *Bradshaw's*, a railway and ship timetable. He took the bag from Passepartout and put a lot of money into it. Then he gave the bag to Passepartout.

'Look after it,' he said. 'There's twenty thousand pounds in it.'

At the station, Phileas Fogg saw his five friends from the Reform Club.

'You're here to say goodbye? That's kind,' he said. 'I'll have **stamp**s in my **passport** for each country. You can see them when I come back.'

'We won't look at your passport,' said Ralph. 'You're an Englishman.'

At 8.40, Phileas Fogg and Passepartout took their places in the train, and at 8.45 the train started.

◆

Some days later, the police at Scotland Yard* had a letter from their detective, Detective Fix.

Suez, 9th October
To Scotland Yard, London
*I am following the bank thief, Phileas Fogg. Send a **warrant** to Bombay now.*
Fix (detective)

---

* Scotland Yard: the central office of London's police detectives.

stamp /stæmp/ (n) When you arrive in a country, you often get a *stamp* with the date in your passport.
passport /ˈpɑːspɔːt/ (n) You show your *passport* when you visit other countries. The name of your country is on the front.
warrant /ˈwɒrənt/ (n) With a *warrant*, the police can take somebody to a police station or go into their house.

2.1 Were you right?

Look back at your answers to Activity 1.2. Circle the right answers.

1 Phileas Fogg has *£20,000 / no money* in the bank.
2 Passepartout is Phileas Fogg's new *friend / servant*.
3 Phileas Fogg has *four / five* friends at his club. Each friend bets *£4,000 / £5,000*.
4 Phileas Fogg has to go round the world in eighty days or he will lose *£4,000 / £20,000*.

2.2 What more did you learn?

What are these people thinking or saying? Write the numbers, 1–5.

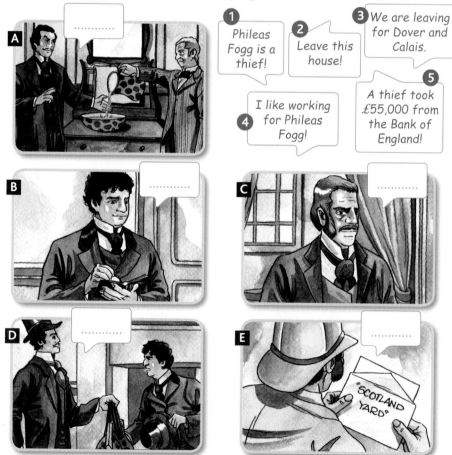

2.3 Language in use

Look at the sentences in the box.
Then use *have to* in these sentences.

> Everything in his life **had to** be right.
>
> We **have to** go now.

1 Phileas Fogg was very angry, so his servant .... find a new job.

2 Passepartout .... take tea to Phileas Fogg at 8.23 every day.

3 'When .... we .... be back in England?' asked Passepartout.

4 'You .... not .... show us the passport stamps when you come back,' Phileas's friends said.

5 'You .... find the thief!' the police told Detective Fix.

6 Phileas Fogg was out all day, so Passepartout .... not .... work very hard.

7 'Phileas Fogg bet a lot of money last night. Why .... he .... bet £20,000?' his friend asked.

8 Phileas Fogg is rich and .... not .... work.

2.4 What happens next?

Look at the pictures in Chapters 3 and 4, the name of Chapter 3 and the words in *italics* below it. What is going to happen (✓)?

		Yes	No
1	Detective Fix and Passepartout will meet.	( )	( )
2	Passepartout will lose Phileas Fogg's money.	( )	( )
3	Passepartout will run away with Phileas Fogg's money.	( )	( )
4	Some men will take Passepartout's shoes.	( )	( )
5	Phileas Fogg and Passepartout will have to leave a train.	( )	( )
6	Phileas Fogg and Passepartout will go on a large animal.	( )	( )
7	Phileas Fogg will meet a beautiful woman.	( )	( )
8	Detective Fix will catch Phileas Fogg.	( )	( )

CHAPTER 3

Detective Fix

He left London quickly. He had a lot of money in new banknotes.
Phileas Fogg was, Fix thought, the Bank of England thief.

O n Wednesday, 9th October a small thin man waited for a ship at Suez, Egypt. The ship, a fast ship, was the *Mongolia*. The man was Detective Fix. He was at the port because he wanted to find the Bank of England thief.

Fix looked at everybody. He wanted a tall man in expensive clothes. When the *Mongolia* arrived at the port, Phileas Fogg left the ship. He had to get a stamp in his passport. He went back to the ship. Fix watched him.

Then the detective found Passepartout out in the town.

'Can I help you?' asked Fix.

'You are very kind,' said Passepartout. 'This is Suez?'

'Yes,' said Fix. 'Suez, in Egypt, in Africa.'

Passepartout looked at Fix with wide eyes.

'Africa!' he said. 'This morning I saw Paris again, from 7.20 to 8.15 in the morning, through the windows of a train, between two railway stations. And now I am here in Africa.'

'You haven't got much time, then?' asked the detective.

'No, Mr Fogg hasn't got much time. Oh, and I have to buy some clothes. We came away with only one small bag for the journey.'

'I'll show you the way to the shops.'

'Thank you,' said Passepartout. And the two men walked through Suez. 'I have to be careful about the time. The ship leaves again in a short time.'

'You've got time for shopping,' Fix answered. 'And you've got time for lunch.'

Passepartout pulled out his big watch.

'Lunch?' he said. 'It's 9.52 in the morning!'

'No, it's 11.52,' said Fix. 'You've got London time on your watch. That's two hours behind Suez time. When you go round the world, time changes. On your journey you'll have to change the time on your watch for each new country.'

'What! Change the time on my watch? Never!' said Passepartout.

Fix smiled. Five minutes later he said, 'Here are the shops. You can buy everything here. I think you left London quickly.'

'Oh yes! Last Wednesday, Mr Fogg came back from his club at 7.50 in the evening. He usually comes back at midnight. And then we started our journey.'

Fix thought about that. Then he asked, 'But where is Mr Fogg going?'

'Round the world.'

'Round the world?'

'Yes, in eighty days. He says it is for a bet.'

'Is he rich?' Fix asked.

'I *think* he is,' said Passepartout. The Frenchman was always ready to talk. 'He has a lot of new banknotes with him, and he buys things all the time. He gave the **captain** of the *Mongolia* a lot of money because he wanted to get to Bombay early.'

So the detective wrote to London and asked for a warrant in Bombay. Phileas Fogg was tall and wore expensive clothes. He left London quickly. He had a lot of money in new banknotes. Phileas Fogg was, Fix thought, the Bank of England thief.

Ten minutes before the *Mongolia* left Suez, Fix was on the ship with a light bag and some money. He was on his way to Bombay.

captain /ˈkæptən/ (n) The *captain* of a ship is the boss.

13

CHAPTER 4

India

'What?' said Phileas Fogg. 'Are you saying that this woman
wants to die with her husband?'

Phileas Fogg looked at the timetable. *'The* Mongolia *will arrive in*
Bombay on 22nd October' he wrote in his little black book.

But she arrived two days early because there was a north-west wind
behind her. He wrote *'two days early'* in the little black book, but he did
not smile.

At 4.30 in the afternoon of 20th October, everybody left the ship and
went into Bombay.

'The train from Bombay to Calcutta leaves at 8 o'clock,' Phileas Fogg
told Passepartout. 'Be at the railway station before then.' Then he went
to the passport office and had dinner at the railway station.

Fix went to the police in Bombay and asked about the warrant. He
could not take Phileas Fogg back to England without a warrant. But the
warrant was not there. It was in the post from England, so Fix could
do nothing.

Passepartout looked at Bombay. Everything was interesting to the young man. He stood outside the fine **temple** at Malabar. He liked it, so he went inside.

But Passepartout didn't know that you can't go into a temple in India in your shoes.

'This temple is really lovely,' thought Passepartout. He looked at the beautiful things in there. Suddenly, three men in orange clothes started to hit him. Then they threw him to the floor and took his shoes. They were very angry. They shouted something, but Passepartout didn't understand the language. But the Frenchman was young and strong. He pushed the men away and ran out of the temple into the street.

At 7.55, five minutes before the train left, Passepartout arrived at the station without his shoes, without a hat, and without the bag of new clothes. He found Phileas Fogg at the dinner table.

temple /ˈtempəl/ (n) A *temple* is a building. There are *temples* in many countries for different gods.

Fix was at the station restaurant too. He sat behind Phileas Fogg and watched him. He listened to Passepartout and Phileas Fogg. Passepartout moved his arms up and down when he told Phileas Fogg about the temple.

The detective smiled. 'So the servant did something wrong in this country,' he thought. 'I can use that. The thief will have to stay in India. And I can wait for the warrant from England.'

◆

Phileas Fogg and Passepartout sat on the train through the night, the next day and the next night. Everything was different outside from one minute to the next minute. Passepartout watched the many changes through the window. They were very interesting to him. Phileas Fogg was not interested.

At 8 o'clock in the morning, on 22nd October, the train stopped near the station at Rothal. A man from the railway came to the train window.

'Everybody, get out of the train, please,' he called.

'Why do we have to get out?' asked Phileas Fogg.

'Because there is no more railway after this. It begins again at Allahabad, about fifty miles from here.'

'But it's in *The Times*,' said Phileas Fogg. He had the centre page of the newspaper with him. 'Look. The paper says *"The railway between Rothal and Allahabad is open now."*'

'The paper is wrong.'

'But your company sells tickets from Bombay to Calcutta,' the Englishman said.

'Oh yes,' the railwayman answered. 'But everybody knows that they have to go from Rothal to Allahabad on foot or on a horse.'

He was right. The other people in the train knew about the railway. They left the train quickly and went to the village. They took all the horses.

'We'll walk,' said Phileas Fogg.

Passepartout looked down at his feet. He didn't have any shoes. His shoes were in the Malabar temple in Bombay.

'There's an **elephant** over there,' he said.

The man with the elephant smiled a wide smile. A man with an elephant is a rich man when there isn't a railway. Phileas Fogg started at ten pounds an hour. No? Twenty? No? Forty? No.

In the end, the man sold the elephant to Phileas Fogg for two thousand pounds.

'Elephant meat is expensive,' Passepartout thought.

Next, they had to find a **guide**. They didn't know the way to Allahabad. That was easier. A young Indian from the village saw them with the elephant.

'Do you want a guide?' he asked. He spoke English too.

Every two hours, the guide stopped the elephant. It ate and drank some water. Phileas Fogg, Passepartout and the guide sat under a tree, out of the sun. Then they started again. They moved quickly, and climbed higher.

---

elephant /ˈeləfənt/ (n) An *elephant* is a very large, grey Indian or African animal with big ears.

guide /ɡaɪd/ (n) A *guide* shows places to visitors. That is his or her job.

By 8 o'clock in the evening, they were over the Vindhia mountains. They were half-way to Allahabad. The guide stopped for the night.

They started again at 6 o'clock the next morning, and at 4 o'clock in the afternoon they were near Allahabad.

They were in some trees when suddenly the elephant stopped. They heard the sound of singing and loud music. The guide drove the elephant into the thickest trees.

'It is a dead man,' said the guide, quietly. 'They are taking a dead man to a temple. Tomorrow they will start a fire and put the dead man on the fire.'

Through the trees, they saw a lot of people. Some men wore the same orange clothes as the three men at the Malabar temple. Some men played music. Some women and children walked behind them. Then they saw a young woman. Some men pushed her in front of them. She was very beautiful, but she was very weak. She couldn't walk very well. Men at the back carried a dead man in fine clothes.

'The dead man was important,' said the guide. 'The young woman was his wife, and they will put her on the fire tomorrow with her dead husband.'

'What?' said Phileas Fogg. 'Are you saying that this woman wants to die with her husband?'

'Sometimes a wife wants to die when her husband dies,' answered the guide. 'But this young woman does not want to die. Those people, the people in the orange clothes, say she has to do it.'

'No!' said Passepartout. 'But can't she get away from them?'

'They put something in her food,' the guide said. 'Look – she is very tired. Then she will sleep.'

'We'll get her out of here,' said Phileas Fogg.

'Please think before you try that,' said the guide. 'These people are dangerous.'

'But, Mr Fogg, the bet ...' said Passepartout.

Phileas Fogg looked at the timetable. 'I am one day early. We can use the day well, and get the young woman away from here.'

'Well,' said the guide. 'We can follow them, but we cannot go too near. They are going to a temple about two miles from here. I know about the young wife too. Her name is Aouda. Her father had a big company in Bombay. But her father and mother died and she had to marry that old man. We cannot do anything now. But I will help you when it gets dark.'

3.1 Were you right?

Look back at Activity 2.4. Then answer the questions.

1 Why does Detective Fix want to catch Phileas Fogg?

....

....

2 Does Detective Fix catch Phileas Fogg in these chapters?

....

3 Why do some men take off Passepartout's shoes?

....

....

4 Why do Phileas Fogg and Passepartout have to leave the train?

....

....

5 Why do they go on an elephant?

....

....

3.2 What more did you learn?

Put the right words in these sentences.

1 Passepartout wants to buy some .... and Fix takes him to the
....

2 .... tells Fix that Phileas Fogg has a lot of ....

3 Phileas Fogg, Passepartout and .... take a ship to ....

4 When Passepartout arrives at the station in Bombay, he has no
....

5 The other people on the train go to Allahabad on ....

6 Phileas Fogg has to pay £2,000 for the ....

7 Aouda's .... is dead and people are going to put him on a
....

8 Aouda does not want to ....with her husband.

3.3 Language in use

Look at the sentences in the box. Then make sentences with *when* and the words below. Use past tense verbs.

> **When** the *Mongolia* **arrived** at the port, Phileas Fogg **left** the ship.
>
> Passepartout **moved** his arms up and down **when** he **told** Phileas Fogg about the temple.

1 ship / arrive / Bombay / everybody / go / city

....

....

2 men / temple / see / Passepartout's shoes / start to hit him

....

....

3 Phileas Fogg / be / at the dinner table / Passepartout / arrive / station

....

....

4 Everybody / have to get out / train / stop

....

....

5 Phileas Fogg / hear about / young Indian woman / want / help her

....

....

3.4 What happens next?

These pictures are from the next chapters of the story. What are the people in the pictures saying, do you think? Talk about it.

CHAPTER 5

Aouda

The old man was not dead. He stood up and took the young woman in his arms.
Then he came down through the fire.

People sang and shouted. The noise came through the trees. The guide stopped the elephant and they walked. They could see the temple, white in the dark night. Some men with guns sat round it and watched.

'The young woman is inside the temple,' said the guide, quietly. The dead man was on top of some wood, to the right. 'When the sun comes up, they will put the woman next to her husband. Then they will start the fire.'

'We'll have to think of something. We have to get the young woman out of there,' said Phileas Fogg.

But Phileas Fogg and the guide did not have any ideas. And the men with guns round the temple did not go to sleep. They watched. They watched very carefully.

After an hour or two the guide said, 'Mr Fogg, where is your servant?'
Phileas Fogg could not answer that. Passepartout was not there.

◆

The sun came up in the east. The people woke and went noisily to the
wood with the dead man on top. Then some men brought Aouda out
of the temple. She did not move when they put her down on top of the
wood, next to her dead husband. There was something in her food again
that morning.

Some men brought fire to the wood. Phileas Fogg stood up and
opened his mouth. He wanted to shout, 'Stop!'

'Get down!' said the guide. 'They will kill us!'

But suddenly everything changed. The people gave a great shout, and
they fell down on their faces with their eyes to the ground.

The old man was not dead. He stood up and took the young woman
in his arms. Then he came down through the fire. He walked over the
people on the ground. Then he carried the woman easily in strong arms
to Phileas Fogg and the guide.

'Let's go!' he said. 'Quickly!'

It was Passepartout.

A minute later, the three men and the young woman were on the elephant. Aouda slept and knew nothing about it.

The sun was high and hot in the sky. It was nearly 10 o'clock in the morning.

The young guide said, 'There, that is Allahabad. The railway starts again there. The train journey to Calcutta is about a day and a night.'

Phileas Fogg took a room at the railway station for Aouda. He sent Passepartout into the town for clothes and other things for the young woman. When the train was ready, Aouda was better.

Before they got in the train, Phileas Fogg paid the guide.

'That's your money, because you were our guide,' he said. 'But you helped us in other ways. Would you like the elephant?'

The young guide gave a big smile. That was his only answer.

On the journey to Calcutta, Aouda learned about her night in the temple and about Passepartout and the fire. She said 'Thank you' again and again, but she was afraid of her husband's family. She didn't want them to catch her again.

'I'll take you to Hong Kong,' Phileas Fogg said, 'and you can stay there.'

It was kind, but he spoke quite coldly.

She happily said, 'Oh, thank you! I have an uncle in Hong Kong. He will look after me.'

The train got to Calcutta at 7 o'clock in the morning. Phileas Fogg had five hours before the ship left for Hong Kong.

CHAPTER 6

Calcutta

Passepartout felt bad. ... 'A bet of twenty thousand pounds,' he thought.
'And we will lose it, because I went into a temple in shoes!'

P hileas Fogg, Passepartout and Aouda left the station at Calcutta.
They wanted to go to the passport office and then to the ship. But a
policeman came to them and said: 'Are you Mr Phileas Fogg, and is this
your servant?'

'Yes.'

'Please follow me.'

Phileas Fogg's face did not change. He didn't feel anything, or he
didn't show it.

'Can this young woman come with us?' he asked.

The policeman said, 'Yes.'

At the police station, the policeman took them to a large room with a
big cupboard in it. Then the three men in orange clothes from the Malabar
temple in Bombay came in. One man carried Passepartout's shoes.

'The temple in Bombay!' said Passepartout.

The men from the temple were in Calcutta because Fix brought them from
Bombay. Fix told the Calcutta police about the Malabar temple. Now, he was
in the big cupboard in the room, and he listened to everything.

The policeman said, 'People from other countries cannot come to
India and wear their shoes in a temple. It is not right. You will have to
stay in **prison**. You can tell your story next week. Then perhaps you will
have to stay in prison.'

Fix was very happy about that. 'The warrant will arrive before then,'
he thought.

Passepartout felt bad. He was not afraid of prison, but he thought of
Phileas Fogg and his bet. 'A bet of twenty thousand pounds,' he thought.
'And we will lose it, because I went into a temple in shoes!'

---

prison /ˈprɪzən/ (n) A *prison* is a building. Killers have to live in *prison* for years before they
can leave.

Phileas Fogg's face did not change. He said: 'I want bail.'

'Yes, you can have **bail**,' said the policeman.

Fix, in the cupboard, was angry.

'But,' the policeman said, 'because you do not live in this country, bail will be one thousand pounds each. You will have to come back here in a week, and then you will get your money back. You can tell your story then.'

Fix was happy about that. He thought, 'Fogg won't pay two thousand pounds of bail money. He'll stay in prison and wait.' To Fix, Phileas Fogg was a bank thief, not a man with a twenty thousand pound bet.

'I'll pay,' said Phileas Fogg.

'You will get this money back,' said the policeman, 'when you come back next week. But now you can go, on bail.'

Passepartout turned to the three men from the temple. 'Please,' he said, 'give me my shoes back.'

The Frenchman put on his shoes again. Then Fogg, Aouda and Passepartout went to the port as quickly as they could. Fix followed. He was very angry. 'That's two thousand pounds of the Bank of England's money,' he thought. 'I'll have to take Fogg back to England quickly.'

---

bail /beɪl/ (n) When you pay *bail* money, you can leave prison. You are then on *bail*. Later, you will have to go to court or you will lose the money.

4.1 Were you right?

Look back at your sentences in Activity 3.4. Then read the sentences below. Are they right (✓) or wrong (✗)?

1 The men put Aouda on the wood for the fire. ◯

2 Passepartout puts on the dead man's clothes. ◯

3 Passepartout, Phileas Fogg and the guide leave
   Aouda near the temple. ◯

4 The men from the temple in Bombay come to Calcutta. ◯

5 Passepartout thinks that Phileas Fogg will lose his bet. ◯

6 Fix thinks that Phileas Fogg will pay the bail money. ◯

7 Phileas Fogg pays £1,000 bail money. ◯

4.2 What more did you learn?

Answer the questions. Write the letters, A–E.

1 Who gives away an elephant? ◯

2 Who thanks Phileas Fogg many times? ◯

3 Who has an uncle in Hong Kong? ◯

4 Who takes Phileas Fogg to a police station? ◯

5 Who listens from a cupboard? ◯

6 Who asks for some shoes? ◯

4.3 Language in use

Look at the sentences in the box. Then write a sentence or question with *will* about each picture.

> 'Get down!' said the guide. 'They **will kill** us!'
>
> 'I have an uncle in Hong Kong. He **will look after** me.'

1 ....
....
....

2 ....
....
....

3 ....
....
....

4 ....
....
....

5 ....
....

4.4 What happens next?

In the next chapters, who says these words, do you think? Write the names.

'Will you take me to Yokohama?'

1 ....

'Who do you think I am?'

2 ....

'Come to Europe.'

3 ....

'I will kill Fix!'

4 ....

CHAPTER 7

Hong Kong

*'Who do you think I am?' 'You are working for those five men
from the Reform Club,' smiled Passepartout.*

On the ship to Hong Kong, the *Rangoon*, Aouda learned a little
about Phileas Fogg. She liked him.

Fix was on the ship too. He thought about the warrant. Was it now on
its way from Bombay to Hong Kong?

On the first day, Passepartout did not know that Fix was on the ship
too. But then he saw the detective.

'What is Mr Fix doing on this ship?' the Frenchman thought. 'We
saw him in Suez and now here he is again. Is he following us? Why?'
Passepartout thought about it, and then he had an idea. 'He is following
Mr Fogg. He is working for the five men at the Reform Club. He is
watching Mr Fogg because of the bet.'

Passepartout was angry with the five men, but he didn't tell Phileas Fogg about Fix. The five men were Mr Fogg's friends. Passepartout didn't want Mr Fogg to think badly of them. He really liked Mr Phileas Fogg now. He wanted him to win his bet. It was important to him.

◆

The weather was bad and the *Rangoon* arrived at Hong Kong twenty-four hours late. Phileas Fogg, Passepartout and Aouda went to the office of the ship company.

'Are we too late for the *Carnatic*?' Phileas Fogg asked. 'The timetable says she left Hong Kong for Yokohama yesterday.'

'No,' said the man at the office. 'The *Carnatic* had a problem with one **engine**. She's here. She'll leave tomorrow.'

'Thank you,' said Phileas Fogg.

Phileas Fogg took Aouda to the best hotel in Hong Kong. Then he went out and looked for her uncle. An hour later, he came back. Aouda's uncle did not live in Hong Kong now. He was in Holland.

engine /ˈendʒɪn/ (n) When its *engine* doesn't work, a car doesn't move.

Aouda did not speak for a minute. She sat with her head in her hands. Then, very quietly, she asked, 'What do I do now, Mr Fogg?'

'That's easy,' said Phileas Fogg. 'Come to Europe.'

'But I will be one more problem for you ...'

'You're not a problem. And you won't change our timetable. Passepartout?'

'Yes, Mr Fogg?'

'Go to the *Carnatic*, Passepartout, and get three tickets to Yokohama.'

Passepartout left the hotel with a smile on his face. He wanted to have Aouda with them on the journey. She always spoke kindly to him. To her, he was a friend and not a servant.

When Passepartout arrived at the port, he saw a very unhappy Fix by the *Carnatic*.

Fix was unhappy because the warrant was in the post from Bombay and not in Hong Kong. The *Carnatic* could take Phileas Fogg away from Hong Kong before the warrant arrived. Passepartout smiled at Fix's face.

'The fine, rich men of the Reform Club are going to lose their money,' the Frenchman thought, 'and Mr Fix is unhappy about that.'

'Are you going to buy a ticket for the *Carnatic*?' asked Passepartout. He laughed, but Fix said nothing.

The Frenchman went onto the *Carnatic*, and paid for three tickets to Yokohama. The *Carnatic*'s captain spoke to him.

'The engine is fine now,' he said. 'The problem was smaller than we thought. The ship will leave at 8 o'clock this evening. Not tomorrow.'

'Good,' said Passepartout. 'I will tell my Mr Fogg. He will be happy.' When he left the ship, Fix came to him.

'Before you see Mr Fogg,' said Fix, 'won't you have a drink with me in this bar?'

There was a bar at the port, near the ships.

'Well, yes, thank you. I am quite thirsty,' the Frenchman said.

In the bar, Fix asked Passepartout, 'Who do you think I am?'

'You are working for those five men from the Reform Club,' smiled Passepartout. 'You are watching Mr Fogg.'

Fix thought for a minute. He didn't have the warrant, and he had to stop Fogg.

'Yes, I am watching Fogg,' said Fix. 'But I'm not working for the men from the club. I'm a policeman. I'm following Fogg because he's a bank thief. You have to help me, or I'll get a warrant for you too. I'll put you in prison with him. Now, are you with me or are you with him?'

Passepartout was angry. 'With him,' he said, and he started to leave the bar.

Passepartout was on his way back to Phileas Fogg. Fix had to stop him. Passepartout knew about the ship's new timetable, and Phileas Fogg didn't. So Fix put something in Passepartout's drink.

'Wait!' called Fix. He smiled. 'Why don't you finish your drink before you go? It's hot out there.' Fix smiled again.

Passepartout stopped. He looked angrily at Fix but he took the drink. He sat down and finished it. Then he quietly went to sleep in his chair.

Fix left him in the bar.

CHAPTER 8

To Japan?

They saw a big American ship coming a little way out of the port.
'Too late!' cried the seaman. 'Your ship is leaving.'

Phileas Fogg took Aouda to the best shops in Hong Kong. They went from one shop to another shop. He pulled money out of his bag and bought her dresses and other clothes. Then they went back to the hotel.

Night came and there was no Passepartout. In the morning, too, Passepartout was not there. Phileas Fogg and Aouda went to the port. Perhaps Passepartout was at the ship. But the servant was not there and the *Carnatic* was also not there.

An Englishman spoke to Phileas Fogg. 'Did you have tickets for the *Carnatic*?' The man was Fix. 'I wanted to go to Yokohama on the *Carnatic* too,' the detective said. 'She left yesterday evening. We'll have to wait a week for the next ship.'

Fix smiled. But the detective's smile left him when Phileas Fogg said: 'But there are other ships in the port of Hong Kong. The *Carnatic* is not the only ship. Let's go and find one.'

Phileas Fogg looked for a ship for a long time. Ships arrived and stayed. Ships left before he could speak to anybody on them.

'Are you looking for a boat?' asked a seaman.

'Is your boat ready to leave?'

'Yes. It's a small boat. Number 43. Do you know these small boats? They help the big ships when they arrive at the port. And this boat is the best in Hong Kong.'

'Is she fast?

'Oh yes! Eight or nine miles an hour.'

'Will you take me to Yokohama? I had tickets for the *Carnatic* but she left early. I have to be in Yokohama on 14th November. I have to catch the ship for San Francisco there. I can give you a hundred pounds a day, and two hundred pounds more in Yokohama on or before 14th November.'

'But why Yokohama?' said the seaman. 'We can go to Shanghai, only 800 miles from Hong Kong. The ship for San Francisco starts from Shanghai. Then it goes to Yokohama before it goes to America.'

This was very interesting to Phileas Fogg. 'That's not in my *Bradshaw*,' he said. 'Shanghai? And when does the ship for San Francisco leave Shanghai?'

'On 11th November, at seven in the evening. So we have four days. With the wind in the south-east, we can get to Shanghai in four days.'

'When can we start?' asked Phileas Fogg.

'In an hour. We'll get food and water first.'

'Is she your boat? Or a company's?'

'Oh, she's my boat. My name's Bunsby, and the *Tankadere* is mine.'

'Here's two hundred pounds,' said Phileas Fogg. Then he turned to Fix. 'Do you want to come with us?'

'Er, well, I, er ...'

'In half an hour then,' said Phileas Fogg.

'But what about ...' Aouda said. And then she stopped. She was very unhappy about Passepartout but she understood about the bet.

'I'm going to do everything possible for Passepartout,' said Phileas Fogg.

He went with Aouda to the police in Hong Kong. He left a letter about Passepartout and money for his ticket back to Europe.

◆

At 3 o'clock, Phileas Fogg, Aouda and Fix were on the *Tankadere*, and the little boat started her journey to Shanghai. The wind helped, and the boat moved fast, to the north-east. With the wind behind them, they cut through the sea, very near China.

But in the early morning of the second day, the seaman, Bunsby, came to Phileas Fogg.

'There's too much wind now,' he said. 'We get these very high winds near China. They're dangerous.'

Then it started to rain too.

The weather was very bad. The *Tankadere* started to go high up and then down in the sea. Then left and right, up and down in the wind, under a black sky. With the wind behind them and the heavy rain, it was difficult for Bunsby. But the boat did not go down.

Fix was afraid and very unhappy. Aouda watched Phileas Fogg. His face didn't change.

It was night. The wind was worse and the rain was worse. Aouda fell before Phileas Fogg could catch her.

'I'm fine,' cried Aouda. 'Forget about me.'

Bunsby talked to his seamen, and then came to Phileas Fogg.

'Mr Fogg,' he shouted above the noise of the wind and the rain. The seaman's face was wet with rain. 'Mr Fogg, I think that we'll have to find a port in China. We'll have to stop there.'

'Yes,' said Phileas Fogg.

'But which port?' said the seaman.

'I only know one port,' said Phileas Fogg. He spoke quietly, but Bunsby could hear him above the wind and rain. 'Shanghai.'

The next day was better. The sky was blue again. The boat went through the sea faster. At 7 o'clock they were three miles from Shanghai. They saw a big American ship coming a little way out of the port.

'Too late!' cried the seaman. 'Your ship is leaving.'

Phileas Fogg said, 'Use your radio. Say there's a problem. We want their help.'

When the *Carnatic* left Hong Kong for Japan on 7th November, Passepartout was on the ship.

When Fix walked out of the bar in Hong Kong, Passepartout was asleep in his chair. But then a waiter saw him and gave him some water. His head hurt very badly, and he couldn't think. But one word went round and round in his head, '*Carnatic*! *Carnatic*!'

He walked very, very slowly out of the bar. He could see the *Carnatic* from the bar door, and he walked to it. Then he fell down for the last time. The next morning he woke up and he was on the ship.

It was a sunny day, and Passepartout watched the blue sea. He felt better. He went to the ship's office and asked for Phileas Fogg.

But Phileas Fogg was not on the ship. Aouda was not on the ship. Passepartout sat down. 'What happened?' he thought.

And then he remembered. Mr Fogg didn't know the ship's new timetable.

Passepartout thought, 'He will lose the bet because of me! And because of Fix too.' Passepartout remembered the bar in Hong Kong. 'I will kill Fix!' he thought.

Passepartout was on his way to Japan. He could not change that. 'What can I do when I arrive?' he thought. 'I have no money. I have a ticket, so I can eat on the ship – but after that? I'll eat a lot now,' he thought, 'then I won't have to eat in Japan.' So he ate Phileas Fogg's food, Aouda's food and his food too.

On the morning of 13th November, the *Carnatic* arrived in the port of Yokohama.

5.1 Were you right?

Look back at your answers to Activity 4.4. Then finish these sentences.

1 Aouda has to go to Europe because ....
....

2 On the ship to Hong Kong, Passepartout thinks that Fix ....
....

3 Fix tells Passepartout that Fogg ....

4 Phileas Fogg wants a seaman to take him to Yokohama because ....
....

5 Passepartout would like to kill Fix because ....
....

5.2 What more did you learn?

What is wrong with these pictures?

....
....

....
....

5.3 Language in use

Look at the sentences in the box. Then write answers to these questions.

> Phileas Fogg **took** Aouda to the best hotel in Hong Kong.
>
> She always **spoke** kindly to him.

1 What did Phileas Fogg buy?

He ....

....

2 What did Detective Fix do to Passepartout's drink?

He ....

....

3 What did Detective Fix give Passepartout?

He ....

....

4 When did the *Carnatic* leave?

It ....

....

5 Why did Aouda fall in the boat?

She ....

....

5.4 What happens next?

Look at the pictures in the next two chapters and the words in *italics* at the top of page 45. Answer the questions. What do you think?

1 What good things are going to happen?

....

....

2 What problems are Phileas Fogg and Passepartout going to have?

....

....

....

CHAPTER 9

To San Francisco

The warrant was there from Hong Kong but it was too late.
Fix couldn't use the warrant in Japan or America.

Near Shanghai, the captain of the *General Grant* listened to the radio. A smaller boat, *Tankedere*, wanted his help. The American ship stopped next to the *Tankedere*. Phileas Fogg gave Bunsby five hundred and fifty pounds and climbed onto the *General Grant*. He paid for three tickets to San Francisco, and then Aouda and Fix got onto the American ship too.

The first stop was Yokohama. When the *General Grant* arrived there on the morning of 14th November, Fogg and Aouda went to the *Carnatic*. But Passepartout was not there. Phileas Fogg and Aouda looked for Passepartout in the town. They asked questions everywhere. They only had one day before the *General Grant* left for San Francisco. Phileas Fogg and Aouda walked through the streets of Yokohama – north, south, east and west. But they couldn't find Passepartout.

On their way back to the port, they looked in the gardens. There were a lot of gardens in Yokohama. And in the last garden before the port, they saw Passepartout on a chair in the sun. The servant was very happy, and they all went quickly to the *General Grant*.

◆

In Yokohama, Fix went to the police. The warrant was there from Hong Kong but it was too late. Fix couldn't use the warrant in Japan or America.

Passepartout saw Fix on the ship the next day, and the Frenchman hit the detective. Fix fell down on his back.

'Do you feel better?' asked Fix. He got up slowly.

'Yes, for now.'

'Let's talk.'

'Talk?'

'Yes. I want to help your Mr Fogg now.'

'Oh!' said Passepartout. 'So now you know that Mr Fogg is not a thief.'

'No. He's a thief and I have a warrant for him.' Passepartout started to hit him again, so Fix said quickly, 'Wait! I can't use the warrant here. But Mr Fogg is going to England. I can use the warrant there. So I want to help him. He wants to get to England quickly, and I want him to get there too. So I can help you now, and you can help me. We can be friends.'

'Friends? Never!' said Passepartout. 'But you can help Mr Fogg. That's fine.'

'I'll help him. A Scotland Yard detective can do a lot of things. But don't tell him about the bar in Hong Kong. And don't say I'm a detective. Then I'll help him.'

Passepartout thought hard but said nothing.

The *General Grant* had the wind behind her and a good engine too. On 3rd December, she went through the Golden Gate and into San Francisco.

CHAPTER 10

Across America

They heard guns and shouts. Passepartout looked out of the window.
The Indians were on fast horses.

They had to wait for the train from San Francisco to New York. It left at 6 o'clock in the evening.

Phileas Fogg went with Aouda and got a stamp in his passport. Passepartout bought guns for the railway journey. The Sioux Indians were dangerous.

At 5.45, Phileas Fogg, Aouda and Passepartout were at the station. The train was ready. And there was Fix again! Phileas Fogg couldn't understand it.

They all got on the train. The journey time was seven days. Phileas Fogg wanted to catch a ship from New York to Liverpool on 11th December.

On the first day, at about 3 o'clock in the afternoon, Passepartout looked out of the window and saw some **buffaloes**. He saw hundreds of the big animals, and then thousands of them. They walked in front of the train and the train had to stop.

Some people on the train were angry because the train had to  stop on a hot day. They had to sit there and wait. But Phileas Fogg wasn't angry. He didn't look at his watch. He sat quietly and waited. In three hours, the thousands of buffaloes moved slowly across the railway, and then the train could start again.

buffalo /ˈbʌfələʊ/ (n) *Buffaloes* are North American, Asian or African animals. When they work for people, they usually pull things.

The next morning, everybody on the train heard the Sioux Indians. They heard guns and shouts. Passepartout looked out of the window. The Indians were on fast horses. They wanted to get on the train and take everybody's money. But a lot of people on the train had guns and they fought.

A Sioux Indian killed the train driver. The Sioux wanted to stop the train but he did not understand the engine. The train went faster, not slower.

They were very near the station at Fort Kearney, and there were **soldiers** there. The people on the train wanted to stop the train at the station. Then the soldiers could help them. But somebody had to get to the engine and stop the train.

Passepartout called, 'I will go!'

He climbed out of the window and then climbed under the train to the engine. The Indians didn't see him. Then Passepartout stopped the engine quite near Fort Kearney.

Other people from the train walked to Fort Kearney and talked to the soldiers. The soldiers came back to the train. The Sioux ran away, but

soldier /ˈsəʊldʒə/ (n) *Soldiers* fight for their country.

they took three people from the train with them. Passepartout was one of the three.

Aouda started to cry, but Phileas Fogg said to her, 'I'll get him back.'

The captain gave Phileas Fogg thirty soldiers, and they went after the Indians. Fix wanted to go with Phileas Fogg, but Phileas Fogg said, 'Please stay here and look after Aouda.'

He walked away, and Aouda watched him. It started to snow.

More and more snow fell out of a dark sky. Phileas Fogg and the thirty soldiers did not come back that day or the next night. Fix and Aouda waited at Fort Kearney, but the train left without them.

The next morning, Fix, Aouda and the soldiers at Fort Kearney heard a shout. The thirty soldiers were back with Phileas Fogg, Passepartout and the two other people from the train.

'The train left without us,' Fix told Phileas Fogg. 'The next train is this evening.'

But that was too late. Phileas Fogg was now twenty hours behind his timetable. They could not arrive in New York by train before their ship, the *China*, left.

6.1 Were you right?

Look back at Activity 5.4. Then circle the right answers below.
Sometimes, there is more than one right answer.

1 Phileas Fogg and Aouda find Passepartout ...
   a in a garden.   **b** in a street.   **c** on the *Carnatic*.

2 The *General Grant* takes Phileas Fogg and his friends to ...
   a Yokohama.   **b** San Francisco.   **c** New York.

3 Buffaloes stop the train to New York for ...
   a two hours.   **b** three hours.   **c** five hours.

4 Indians take away ...
   a Phileas Fogg.   **b** Passepartout.   **c** three people.

5 Phileas Fogg comes back with ...
   a thirty soldiers.   **b** Passepartout.   **c** some Indians.

6.2 What more did you learn?

What happens first? Number these 1–10.

a Buffaloes stop the train to New York.

b Fix tells Passepartout that he will help Phileas Fogg.

c The train leaves without Phileas Fogg and his friends.

d Indians take away Passepartout.

e Passepartout hits Fix.

f Phileas Fogg, Aouda and Fix climb onto the *General Grant*.

g Phileas Fogg and Aouda find Passepartout.

h Phileas Fogg and the soldiers come back with Passepartout.

i Passepartout stops the train.

j Fix gets his warrant.

6.3 Language in use

Look at the sentences on the right.
Then write some of the words from
the box in the sentences below.

> They asked questions
> **everywhere.**
>
> But **somebody** had to
> get to the engine.

somebody	anybody	everybody	nobody
something	anything	everything	nothing
somewhere	anywhere	everywhere	nowhere

1   We can't find
Passepartout
....

2   ....
could stop the
buffaloes.

3   ....
has to stop the train!

4   We want money from
.... on
the train.

6.4 What happens next?

What will happen (✓) at the end of the story? What do you think?

		Yes	No
1	Phileas Fogg will arrive on time and win his bet.	◯	◯
2	Fix will take Phileas Fogg to a police station.	◯	◯
3	Phileas Fogg will hit Fix.	◯	◯
4	Aouda will find her uncle.	◯	◯
5	Aouda will marry Phileas Fogg.	◯	◯
6	Aouda will marry Passepartout.	◯	◯

CHAPTER 11

Across the Atlantic

'I sent for you, Captain, because I want to buy your ship.'
'No! No! No!'

How could Phileas Fogg win his bet now? No ship in his book of ship and train timetables could get him to London by 21st December.

In New York, Phileas Fogg looked round the port for a fast ship. He wanted to buy one. He saw the *Henrietta*, and spoke to the captain.

'Are you leaving New York, Captain?'

'In an hour,' said the captain. He was a hard man, and his answer was unfriendly.

'Where are you going?'

'To Bordeaux.'

'Can you take us with you?'

'No, I don't take people. Look in *Bradshaw* for a nice ship. I take things from port to port.'

'Fast?' asked Phileas Fogg. 'Do you take things fast?'

'Yes. Very fast. The *Henrietta* does twelve miles an hour.'

'Will you take me, and three other people, to Liverpool, Captain ... What's your name?'

'My name's Speedy and the answer's no!'

'Then I'll buy the ship from you.'

'No!'

Phileas Fogg thought for a minute. Then he said, 'Will you take us to Bordeaux? I can give you two thousand dollars.'

'For each person?'

'Yes.'

Captain Speedy thought about it. Eight thousand dollars!

'We're leaving at nine,' he said.

Phileas Fogg, Aouda, Passepartout and Fix were on the ship when she left New York at 9 o'clock.

The next day, 13th December, Phileas Fogg was captain of the ship. Captain Speedy was in his room, and two seamen watched him carefully. He couldn't leave the room. He shouted, but he couldn't get out.

What happened on that day was this: Phileas Fogg wanted to go to Liverpool. The captain didn't want to go there, but the seamen hated their captain. And Phileas Fogg gave them some money, so they were happy about the new plan.

Now the captain had to stay in his room. Aouda was not very happy about it, but Passepartout enjoyed it.

Phileas Fogg was a very good ship's captain. Perhaps he was a seaman when he was younger. With her fast engine, and the wind behind her, the *Henrietta* moved quickly over the water.

But one of the seamen said, 'Mr Fogg, this engine can take us faster. We have to put more wood on the fire.'

'And where do we get more wood?'

'From the ship. They built everything on it from wood.'

'Thank you,' said Phileas Fogg. 'I'll have to think about it.' He walked round the ship looking at the wood. Then he called Passepartout. 'Bring Captain Speedy to me.'

Captain Speedy ran to Phileas Fogg. He wanted to kill him.

'Thief!' he shouted. 'You took my ship! Where are we?'

'Seven hundred and seventy miles from Liverpool,' said Fogg. 'But I sent for you, Captain, because I want to buy your ship.'

'No! No! No!'

'I'm going to put some of it on the fire, so the engine can take us to Liverpool faster.'

'My ship! This ship cost fifty thousand dollars!'

'Here's sixty thousand,' said Phileas Fogg, and he gave the captain the money. Twelve thousand pounds.

'Oh!' Captain Speedy was suddenly a different man. The *Henrietta* cost fifty thousand dollars, but she was twenty years old.

'You, er ... You only want the wood. I'll have the engine, the ...'

'Oh yes. I'm only buying the wood.'

'Thank you,' said the captain.

And so, at 11.40 on 21st December, Phileas Fogg put his foot on the ground in Liverpool. And at 11.41, Fix said, 'Phileas Fogg, I'm a Scotland Yard detective. Please come with me to the nearest police station.'

CHAPTER 12

The End of the Journey

Phileas Fogg moved quickly for the first and last time in his life.
He hit Fix very hard.

Phileas Fogg was in a police station in Liverpool. He looked at his watch. Two o'clock. He had to be at the Reform Club before 8.45.

At 2.33, there was a lot of noise in the police station. The door opened, and Fix ran in. He was red in the face.

'Mr Fogg!' he cried. 'I'm sorry. I'm very, very sorry. A mistake ... My mistake. We have the Bank of England thief in prison. I was on the ship, so I didn't know.'

Then Phileas Fogg moved quickly for the first and last time in his life. He hit Fix very hard. Fix fell on the floor and stayed there.

Passepartout and Aouda came in and they all went quickly to Liverpool railway station. The London train wasn't there. They were too late.

Phileas Fogg paid for a train. They were the only people on it. But when the train arrived in London, the clock showed 8.50. Phileas Fogg was five minutes late.

◆

Aouda and Passepartout were more unhappy about the bet than Phileas Fogg. This fine man had twenty thousand pounds with him at the start of the journey. And now he had one thousand pounds. He also had twenty thousand pounds in Baring's Bank, but he had to pay it to his five friends in the Reform Club.

At home in Savile Row, Phileas Fogg stayed in his room all day. He thought about money and made plans.

At half past seven in the evening, he came down and spoke to Aouda. He was not sad and he was not excited. He looked at Aouda and smiled.

'Aouda,' he said, 'I'm sorry. I brought you to England and now I have these money problems. Are you unhappy now?'

'Unhappy!' said Aouda. She couldn't tell him.

'I was rich before the bet,' said Phileas Fogg. 'I brought you here to a good life, away from your dangerous life in India. But now I don't have much money. But, Aouda, can I give this money to you? Please.'

Aouda stood up. 'I don't want any money, but I want to be with you. I want to be your wife. Please ask me.' She gave him her hand.

Phileas Fogg looked into her beautiful eyes. There was love in them.

'You know?' he asked. 'Do you know that I love you?'

'Yes,' she said.

Phileas Fogg called Passepartout, and he came quickly. Mr Fogg had Aouda's hand in his hand. Passepartout saw that and he was very, very happy.

'Do you think, Passepartout,' Phileas Fogg said, 'that you can speak to Mr Wilson, at my church? Is it too late in the day?'

Passepartout smiled. 'It is never too late,' he said. It was 8.05. 'For tomorrow, Monday?' he asked.

'For tomorrow, Monday,' said Phileas Fogg and Aouda.

◆

Passepartout ran out. At 8.35 he was back. He was red in the face, and he couldn't speak.

'What is it?' asked Phileas Fogg.

'Mr Fogg ... Please ... Mr Fogg, tomorrow ... You and Aouda. Not possible ...'

'Not possible? Why?' asked Phileas Fogg.

'Because tomorrow is Sunday ...'

'Monday,' said Fogg.

'No ... today is Saturday ...'

'No, it isn't.'

'Yes, it is!' cried Passepartout. 'We made a mistake. We arrived in England a day early. But you only have ten minutes. Let's go, Mr Fogg! You will have to run to the Reform Club. You do it in twenty-five minutes every day, but today you have only ten minutes. Run, Mr Fogg, run!'

He pulled Phileas Fogg to the door. Phileas Fogg ran, and he thought about his mistake. Of course! The time changes in every country. When you go round the world to the west, you lose one day. But when you go round the world to the *east*, you have one more day. But now, was he too late? Phileas Fogg ran through London.

Phileas Fogg's friends were at the card table in the Reform Club that evening. When the clock said 8.25, Stuart said, 'In twenty minutes he'll be too late. The last train from Liverpool arrived at 7.23, and the next one arrives at 12.10. We're going to win our bet!'

Nobody said anything. They weren't really happy. They didn't really want to win the bet. They liked Phileas Fogg. So they played cards and said nothing.

'Eight forty-three,' said Stuart.

Two more minutes. The five men looked sadder and sadder. They watched the door and waited.

A **moment** – a very short moment – before 8.45, Phileas Fogg opened the door and said quietly, 'Here I am, my friends.'

◆

'Now I am a rich man again,' said Phileas Fogg, 'so I'll ask you again. Do you want to be my wife?'

'Yes,' said Aouda. 'But you were a poor man when you asked me. And now you're a rich man again, so do you want to be my husband?'

Passepartout did not wait for the answer. He ran to the church and told Mr Wilson.

moment /'məʊmənt/ (n) A *moment* is a very short time.

1 **Work with three other students. You are going to be one of these people, in the police station in Liverpool. What are you going to say? Think and make notes. Then have the conversation.**

Student A	You are the policeman. Listen and ask questions.

Student B	You are Fix. You are a Scotland Yard detective! Show your warrant and tell the policeman about Phileas Fogg.

Student C	You are Aouda. You want to help Phileas Fogg. Tell the policeman about him.

Student D	You are Passepartout. You want to help Phileas Fogg. Tell the policeman about him.

2 **Work with other students. Discuss these questions.**

A Which person in the story did you like best? Why?

I liked ... best because he/she is ... . Also, he/she ... When..., he/she ...

B Which chapter did you like best? Why?

I liked the chapter about ... . In that chapter, ... Then, ... It was very ... .

C Which country in the story would you like to visit? Why?

I'd like to visit ... because it is ... . I love ... and I enjoy ... .

1 A newspaper hears about Phileas Fogg's bet. The paper wants Passepartout to write about the journey. Make notes for his story.

Phileas Fogg (Is he tall? Is he rich? Is he clever?)

....

Phileas Fogg's bet (What was it? How/where did it happen?)

....

....

You (Passepartout) (Where are you from? What was your work before? What do you do now?)

....

....

The journey (How did you go? Where did you go?)

....

....

Two or three of the problems (What happened? What did you or Mr Fogg do?)

....

....

....

....

The end of the journey (What happened in Liverpool? Did Mr Fogg win his bet? What happened next?)

....

....

....

....

....

2 Now write Passepartout's story in your notebook, with a picture or a map of the journey.

1 Work with another student. You are going to go away for six months in a small bus. You have £2,500 each. Talk about your journey.

- Which country/countries will you visit?
- Which cities will you visit?
- What do you want to see or do there?
- Will you go across the sea?
- How long will you stay in each place?

2 Draw a map of your journey.

3 You want two more people to go with you. Write an advertisement for a student magazine about your journey. Where and when are you going? Give your names and a phone number.

Call Now: 012-ADSPACE

TRAVEL FAST!

4 **Work with four other students. They answered your advertisement and now you are going to talk to them.**

Students A and B	Ask the other four people questions. Which two do you want to go with?

Student C	You are quiet and friendly. You are young for your age. You are at university and you are very clever.

Student D	You like talking. You laugh and tell funny stories. You are very friendly. You left school when you were sixteen. Now you are a cook in a restaurant.

Student E	You are nice and you love visiting other countries. You went to some interesting places last year. You finished university, but you haven't got a job.

Student F	You are Student E's boyfriend/girlfriend. You aren't very friendly, but you really want to get away from your home town. You haven't got much money.

5 **You can only take one bag, and some things for the back of the bus. What will you take with you on your journey? Why? Make notes. Then tell the class. Are you taking different things? Why?**

Notes

6 **Write an email to a friend. Tell your friend about your journey. Answer these questions in your email:**

- When are you going?
- Where are you going?
- What interesting places are you going to visit?
- How are you going to go?
- How long are you going to stay in each place?

- Who are you going to go with?
- How did you find them?
- What are you going to take?
- How do you feel about the journey?
- How does your family feel?
- When will you write again?

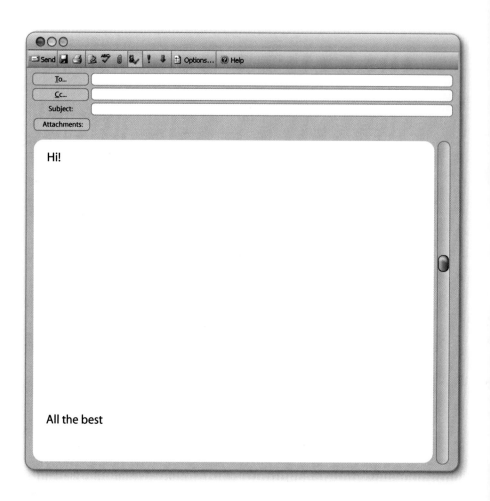

Send | Options... | Help

To...

Cc...

Subject:

Attachments:

Hi!

All the best